THE WORLD WAR II PIGEONS

AND

THE SECRET COLUMBA MESSAGES

The World War II Pigeons and the Secret Columba Messages
All Rights Reserved.
Copyright © 2018 Jennifer Spangler
v4.0

The opinions expressed in this manuscript are solely the opinions of the author and do not represent the opinions or thoughts of the publisher. The author has represented and warranted full ownership and/or legal right to publish all the materials in this book.

This book may not be reproduced, transmitted, or stored in whole or in part by any means, including graphic, electronic, or mechanical without the express written consent of the publisher except in the case of brief quotations embodied in critical articles and reviews.

Outskirts Press, Inc.
http://www.outskirtspress.com

ISBN: 978-1-4787-9211-6

Library of Congress Control Number: 2017914383

Cover and Interior Photos © 2018 National Archives. All rights reserved - used with permission.

Outskirts Press and the "OP" logo are trademarks belonging to Outskirts Press, Inc.

PRINTED IN THE UNITED STATES OF AMERICA

THE WORLD WAR II PIGEONS

AND

THE SECRET COLUMBA MESSAGES

Jennifer Spangler

Acknowledgements

Many thanks to Stewart Wardrop of the Royal Pigeon Racing Association for sending me the wonderful tribute book to the World War I pigeons created by *Racing Pigeon International* and for suggesting I read Peter Hawthorne's *The Animal Victoria Cross-The Dickin Medal* and David Long's *The Animals' VC*.

Paul Johnson of the Image Library and the staff of the Record Copying Department at The National Archives, Kew, made this book possible by answering questions and copying hundreds of documents. Some of the documents are legal size. The Outskirts Press production staff cropped them to fit letter size pages.

Many people were helpful in a variety of significant ways including everybody at Ace Hardware, Fran Berger, Gretchen Beuhler, Barrie Blum at Copy Express, Bob Burns, Tom and Sue Curtin, Henry Damon, Valerie Dumitrescu, Drew Gilpin Faust, Irene Field, Pat Frankel, Ryan Hamilton, David Harris, Shawn Huettner at the UPS store, Carly Huggins, John Kolezar, David Long, Charles Maier, Don and Jan McDowell, Patrick McDowell, Phyllis and Robin Needham, Bernard O'Connor, Michael O'Connor, Macie, Michelle, Jean, Jaimie, Mikey, Sergio, Doug and the entire staff at the Safeway in Fountain Hills, Dora Truong, and Pamela Williams.

Although I am identified as the author, the real authors are the message writers.

Dedicated to veterans and those who put themselves in harm's way.

TOP SECRET.

SPECIAL SECTION (CARRIER PIGEON) R. SIGNALS (Regent 8131/53)

Message No. 963

Pigeon No. 43 - 1549 Sent from Cambridge on 30th July 1944
Returned to Bournemouth on 12th August 1944
Message in French from CHARTRES AREA (EURE ET LOIR) dated 2nd August 1944
Transmitted to S.H.A.E.F.; M.I.14(d), A.I.1(c) at 1600 hours on 12th August 1944

Dear Friends,

It was with great pleasure that we found your pigeon with parachute in very good condition on the 31st July in the plain of BEAUCE (Eure et Loir) district CHARTRES. To show you our devotion and not forgetting our duty to our Fatherland, we will tell you what we know about the enemy although here it is difficult to move about at will on account of the fact that everything has been stolen including our bicycles.

<u>Enemy Defences.</u>   Important Ack-Ack batteries around the town of CHARTRES. Also several searchlights and listening-in posts. Airfield at ETAMPES. Ack-Ack and searchlights at MONDESIR.

<u>Enemy Troops.</u>   HOUVILLE LA BRANCHE. German hospital in the Chateau Boville le Comte. Soldiers of different regiments are being re-grouped at OYSONVILLE on the boundary between SEINE ET OISE and EURE ET LOIR. There are many troops at the Chateau.

Military convoys pass during the night and very early in the morning before six o'clock. They are composed of light armoured cars and lorries. They pass chiefly on the roads from DOURDAN, MONDOUVLEAU, CHARTRES, LIMON, ANGERVILLE, PARIS-ORLEANS, CHARTRES-ORLEANS. Those roads follow roughly the railway lines. The convoys are only lightly escorted.

Kommandantur and Feldgendarmerie and Gestapo at CHARTRES.

Etat Major at AUNEAU.

contd.

SECRET.

Continuation of Report No. 963 - 2 -

The morale of the elderly Germans is fairly low, that of the young ones a bit higher.

Aviation. From the old French aerodromes at CHARTRES, MONDESIR, ETAMPES, bombers of the Junker 88 type depart often in the evening at 8 o'clock at a low altitude in a north-westerly direction.

Works have just been completed 10 kilometres before AUNEAU on the road from CHARTRES to AUNEAU.

In the forest of BARONVILLE there are at the moment fighters which are camouflaged. The types of fighters in that wood have as insignia a yellow flag at the end of the wings and on the rudder.

Many ammunition depots in the forests of Senonches, RANBOUILLET, BAILLEAU L'EVEQUE. There are very important cement block-houses there spaced 500 Kilometres one from the other. They number about 20.

At CHATEAUDUN and at AUNEAU there is a depot of engineering material situated 2 Kilometres from the station of AUNEAU.

B.B.C. On account of lack of electric current, we cannot often listen-in. When we can, we do so in the morning about 0330 hours which is much less jammed than at other times. We do not know any jamming stations.

We very much hope that your pigeon will arrive safely and will be happy if you would let us know of its arrival. We await you impatiently and hope to see you soon to get rid of the dirty Boches who have poisoned our country for 4 years now.

Vive la France et ses Allies.

This comes from a small locality 30 Kilometres from CHARTRES and is sent you by two good Frenchmen of 22 years of age.

(Sgd.) Lulu et Riri.

Pictured to the left is a message written by Lulu and Riri and delivered by pigeon number 43-1549 on August 12, 1944 during Operation Columba. It was transmitted to SHAEF, Supreme Headquarters Allied Expeditionary Force, to M.I.14, the branch of British Military Intelligence responsible for all pigeon-related espionage, and to A.I.1 (c), the Air Intelligence component of M.I.6, the Secret Intelligence Service. The British created Operation Columba to gather intelligence on the Germans in occupied France, Holland, and Belgium. Between 1941 and 1945, approximately 17,000 pigeons were dropped from British planes in baskets, cardboard cages, or containers attached to small parachutes. People sent messages back with the pigeons even though sending a message with a pigeon was a crime punishable by death. Below is a picture of the envelope which contained a questionnaire, rice paper, and a pencil. The instructions tell the finder to hide or destroy the parachute and take the pigeon home or to a safe place.

The Imperial War Museum's Collections has interviews with two men who flew on the pigeon drops, John Douglas Charrot, a Britsh NCO who served as navigator with 138 (Special Duties) Squadron, RAF, in Great Britain from 1941 to 1943, and Frank Cromwell Griffiths, a British officer who served as pilot and flight commander with 138 (Special Duties) Squadron in Great Britain in 1943.

Roderick Bailey includes an excerpt from Charrot's interview in *Forgotten Voices of the Secret War*, "We had a chute you could use as a toilet, a little chute, and we had these bundles of leaflets. It was usually the rear-gunner's job or the wireless operator's, they would tear the string off them and push them down the chute and they would float away. The pigeons we were much more careful about. They had their own little parachute, they were in a little cage made of cardboard and they had food and some water in there, and we used to try and find a nice quiet spot for these so they would be alright. We would drop them and watch them go down and sometimes quite useful information came back, I gather. We didn't see that of course. But there'd be a little pencil in this cage and a piece of rice paper and they were supposed to get hold of these pigeons, you see, write a message and put it round their legs and send them back." According to David Long, writing in *The Animals' VC*, Charrot reported years after his retirement that his squadron alone delivered 39,000 containers of pigeons and 1000 agents. Charrot is referring to pigeons used by Resistance workers and agents, as well as pigeons who participated in Operation Columba.

In his interview, Griffiths reveals that sometimes the men doing the pigeon drops did become aware of what intelligence had been delivered by the pigeons. The pigeons were dropped in country areas, hopefully to be found by civilians who would then send back information. He explains that they didn't drop the pigeons in city areas because people wouldn't pick them up. They were afraid to be seen with a pigeon by the Germans or by a whistleblower. Griffiths discusses a message from Argentan, a small town about 10 miles inland from the Normandy Beaches. The message, sent anonymously, said that the baker in the town was a collaborator. It also contained a description of a telephone exchange being constructed. After the agents on the ground confirmed the information, Griffiths says they "took out" the baker. He says they "took out" the telephone exchange, which was also a headquarters for coastal defenses, just before D-Day. Griffiths adds, "We got a lot of good information on the pigeons."

SECRET.   Message No. 46

SIGS. I [A]—CARRIER PIGEON SERVICE.   Regent 8131/53

Pigeon No. .... Sent from .... on 1941
Returned to .... on .... Brittany 1941
With following Message in French from St Pierre/Dives dated 12.7. 1941
Transmitted to M.I.14, D.N.I. & R.A.F. at .... hours on 14.7. 1941

St Perre/Dives 1th July 1941

How happy I am, in writing these words to be able to help you in a concrete manner, and why do my broken wings prevent me from accompanying the faithful messenger which we are cherishing as one of our soldiers. (I have even taken its photograph).

(1) Here there is no question of invasion. The important concentrations have disappeared. No more practice embarkations no more boats no more rafts. The region is very emptied of Germans and one hopes that soon you will take their place.

(2) No much equipment. Flying ground of St Sylvain Fierville in the wood all round the road crossing of Hill 79 (all the Hills mentioned are those marked on the Etat major map). Important installations hidden in the woods very few bombs - Petrol tanks full - Installations ready but no planes. Last Stukas Squadrons with a black..........hound on a green, red, yellow or white. Left in January.

Flying grounds Ernes Tilly in the woods above the farm of bois Tilly (E.M.map) Installations ready hidden under the woods - petrol - no planes but room for 70 Stukas - bombs ??. The last Stukas carried a shield with the cross of Lorraine above in white on a red ground with below the pilots badge (?) in silver on a blue ground. Left in January.

Percy munitions dump: Installations and buildings all along the railway on the left going from St Pierre to Mezidon from Hill 34 to the station at Mezidon. Important but unknown quantities of munitions. No anti-aircraft defences (D.C.A.) some machine guns on the plateau. Military. St Sylvain 20 - 30 men. Ernes(?) 6 gardes Percy, a small garrison. At St.Pierres Dives be soldiers. The town is reserved for the Air Force which has been expected daily for the last 2 months. Very few soldiers also in the district except at Falaise, about a thousand, In the Mont Eraines between Falaise and Jort fairly frequent firing practices.

(3) A month ago many trains passed with troops and equipment, going towards le Mans. Now there are far fewer: cars - lorries - all light, troops; 7 - 8 daily, especially at night.

(4) St Pierre is, at night, the air centre for regrouping and movements of the JU 88s from Evreux and elsewhere (one brought down in beginning of April 3 died (wounded) (one at the beginning of June J.88 11A, 2 dead)

(6) Bombed night of 9th and 10th, few exact details, hangers damaged and concrete runway (5Km x 50m) Cherbourg bombed very severely. St Remy mines severely damaged. I think it would be a good thing to bomb Percy and damage the flying grounds at Ernes and St Sylvain which are expecting the arrival of planes. Send also leaflets please.

Talking of wireless, we listen regularly, everyone. Just now we hear well on nearly all wave lengths but best on 373m 49m 41m.

The programmes most listened to are 7.15. 1245. 19.15 21.15.
Powerful sets also listen to Brazzoville. Given often French military music we need it so badly.

A fact, to show you how wireless is listened to. One afternoon at 13.10. a young man from our locality was telling about himself. His wife who was listening was very cheered up. 2 minutes had not passed before a dozen or so people arrived to advise her that "Paulo" had given his news, in case she shouldn't have heard it. If you can let him know he will be pleased to know how happy his wife and family are.

B.B.C.

I know that many pigeons get back to you. For my part I am counting on finding others unless as I do so much desire you may have let me know how to get over to you.

To know my name ask Jean and Dennis de Caen, who reached you by air at the beginning of May.

Jean fished me out of the Donlogne the 14th of July 1940.

We are counting on you and we are waiting for you. Victory is with us.

N.B.   The man of St.Sever (Calvados not Landes) who handed over a parachutist, hanged himself for fear of reprisals.

The graves of Engish soldiers are covered with flowers. The others - not.

Mittois 95 found it. Cijogne sends you it.

Please be good enough to announce on the wireless (13.15 ~~preferably~~ preferably) that this message has ~~arrived~~.

Sketch map attached.

found by Mittou 95
sent by Cijogne

SECRET.

SIGS. I [A] — CARRIER PIGEON SERVICE.

Message No. 75.
Regent 8131/53

Pigeon No. DSR 65. Sent from Cambridge on 3rd October 1941
Returned to Folkestone on 4th October 1941
With following Message in French from N. France dated ? 1941
Transmitted to M.I.14 & R.A.F. at 1600 hours on 6th October. 1941

Pigeon was dropped 7 K.M. from the coast (ETAPLES) and was found on the 3rd October.
No troops in this district.
A few at MONTREUIL and no doubt along the coast, but no formations - scattered units but many villages are now without.
Not a single gun or a single tank is seen to go by any more - no G.D.C.A here - about 50 horses with small carts and an equal number of men engaged on transport.
Bad morale with regard to what happens in the East. The soldiers returning from leave come back with their head low and talk of the bombing of Germany.
But their demands are becoming increasing; cows, one talks of horses (?)
It is the destruction of the French breeding stock.
The peasant is requisitioned for more potatoes than he grows and for more grain so that he is left with almost nothing for his own animals.
Discontent is general and one asks one self why, with so few troops to oppose you, there is not a landing on the conquered coast. They cannot claim to be able to resist.
I do not live on the coast.
I cannot get any information about the sea.
I do not want any compensation. One does not need that when one serves one's country.
This is a means for me to avenge myself for my son, whom they have killed.
After the war I would like to replace the pigeons which they have killed, and as I am a lover of pigeons, your one could hardly have come into better hands. I would like to receive some more pigeons to replace those killed.
I come back from a journey.
I have only met troops (trucks) in THEROUANNE, AIRE, ARQUES (Luftwaffe).
Farmers complain of the demands for butter and milk for the Co-operative at Verton and would like to see its disappearance. We would rejoice in its destruction, because there they work for "them".
No more radio (they have broken it), but I would know if you receive this. I will tell a reliable friend who listens in.
No more talk of an invasion of England. They have their hands full with Russia.
All those who talk with me do so with horror. They did not expect such a resistance, and in France neither, so that you are now relegated to second importance. They say that they fear the English soldiers less than the Russians and think that you will not dare ever to make a landing. However if you had good infantry, followed by artillery, to throw on the coast with mechanised units to open the way, you would be surprised. A few scattered soldiers would surrender the rural French as well as the townspeople will rally to your help and are capable of giving you considerable assistance. As hunger is increasing the general discontent grows. Just look at the executions in the "Nord" - but a famished stomach has no ears - and that movement will increase.
No coal for the winter - insufficient and mediocre bread.
When will the end be.
Munition dump at the forest of LONGVILLERS.
When your aeroplanes pass, they become sullen, sad and follow them with glasses.
Petrol dump at the forest of RECQUES on the COURSE.

An ardent A.B.R. 4th Zouaves (bis)

A very dense telephonic network with the central exchange on the right hand side of the National Road No.1, going into MONTREUIL, I think it is the 2nd house. At LE TOUQUET the high authorities live in the very best hotels.

(X) N.B. Wants his pigeons replaced by ords after the war

SECRET. Message No. 64.

SIGS. I A — CARRIER PIGEON SERVICE. Regent 8131/53

Pigeon No. TT 219 Sent from Cambridge on 3rd August 1941
Returned to Ipswich on 12th August 1941
With following Message in French from Courtrai dated 4th August 1941
Transmitted to M.I.14, R.A.F. at 1100 hours on 14th August 1941

There are no preparations being made at the moment for an attack on England.
There are no military movements and no "troupes de combat" in all Belgium or the Département du Nord.
There are men of the navy along the coast and a few aeroplanes and troops at the aerodromes. The same applies to the Pas de Calais.
Here in Belgium and in the North of France there are only occupational troops (without arms), the Gendarmerie, the Gestapo and the German civilians. All fighting units have left the country since the Roumanian campaign and none have returned.
There are no exercises or embarkations being done, and both Officers and men think that Germany will be defeated. They feel very down about their families and the R.A.F. bombardments of Germany.
<u>Aviation.</u> At WEVELGHEM near Courtrai there is an aviation school using the new model Heinschel pursuit planes.
At MOORSEELE near Courtrai there are about 35 Messerschmit pursuit planes in activity.
At BONDUES by Lille are bombers.
The electric power station at COMINES (Nord) is completely at a stand still; the pumping station is destroyed and big damage was done in the interior.
At LIEGE no target was hit, but many civilians were killed.
At BRUSSELS a factory was completely demolished.
At FIVES by Lille a lot of damage was done to works and factories.
We have no reports from the Coast.
The Belgian population is entirely Anglophile, which was proved on the 21st July, when there were numerous manifestations and noisy demonstrations - and also numerous punishments for same.
The REXISTS and the V.N.V. members are known and we have our secret

organisations to deal with them at the opportune moment but we have not m
many arms.
When you come back the whole population will be with you.

Food supplies are difficult and next winter will be hard.
Tuberculosis is making big ravages.
There are frequent demonstrations in the streets for demanding food.
We have to give up 80% of our crops of wheat and potatoes to send to
Germany. They buy up all the vegetables and fruit.

For the following refer to the General Staff map, scale 1 : 50.000,
Sheet 52 - Tourcoing. (Note: See G.S.G.S. Map No.4040).
Map Reference.
783569 ....a wood - munition dump.
775600 ....aerodrome - 35 Messerschmits.
815563 ....   do   - aviation school : Heinschels.
763548 .... a sham aerodrome, illuminated at night.
                                        Wooden dummy planes.
710435 ....aerodrome - bombers.
843560 ....DE COENE works where they are making wooden dummy
                   planes and aerodrome camouflage material.
540595 ....aerodrome, new, under construction,
                                        not yet occupied.

(Sgnd) Bernard Franklin 39.41.

Courtrai 4th August 1941.

Two sketch maps accompany this report and photostat copies are attached.

People risked their lives to send these messages. Under the German occupation, sending a message with a pigeon was a crime punishable by death. Because it was dangerous to have a pigeon, messages had to be written quickly and sent as soon as weather was favorable. Unlike letters, memoirs, or diaries, there wasn't much time for reflection.

TOP SECRET.

SPECIAL SECTION (CARRIER PIGEON) R. SIGNALS (Regent 8131/53)

Message No. 940

Pigeon No. 43-1090   Sent from Cambridge   on 30th July 1944
Returned to Plymouth   on 3rd August 1944
Message in French from LAMBALLE (COTES DU NORD)   dated 2nd Aug. 1944
Transmitted to SHAEF, M.I.14(d),   at 1700 hours on 4th Aug. 1944

In our district of LAMBALLE there are fortifications north and east, trenches, anti-tank walls as well as shelters and barbed wire in every street in the event of invasion. There are also mines.

In the southern part there is an Etat Major with a basement as protection against bombing.

There are heavy guns at BEL-AIR opposite ST.BRIEUC.

Fortunately, there are not many Germans any longer here. They are mostly parachutists, aviators and infantry.

With regard to military convoys, we hardly see any lorries nowadays but only little carts which the farmers are forced, at the peril of their lives, to drive to the front with ammunition. One train passes during the night, fully loaded, often in a northerly direction.

There are still some tanks here, as well as ammunition, about 10 Kms. north as the crow flies.

People say that the Germans can be found in the woods about 2 Kms. south of LAMBALLE. There are also motor cars and taxis there.

With regard to their morale, the old ones are absolutely fed up, whilst the morale of the Hitler Youth is always good. They have a superior air.

1 Km. south of LAMBALLE there is an installation near a small wood on a height. It is alleged to be a transmission post consisting of three deep pits of 80m in the middle of which there is a mast of 30m-40m high, surmounted by a cross. Nearby there are camouflaged houses.

We cannot often listen to the radio because the electric current is cut, and also often jammed, especially in the evening. We had to take our radio sets to the Town Hall, under penalty of death, but some remain. There are three battery sets in our district. News and instructions of the B.B.C. are approved by all except the collaborators.

We live in the hope of being liberated soon. Best greetings.

(Sgd) 5-3

PTO

NEWS DIGEST. 28.3.44.

2.15. De Dag, Antwerp, 23.2.44. reports: "The French subjects Rene Habaut and Paul Pavot have been sentenced to death by Court-Martial for espionage and have been shot. Habaut and Pavot had attempted to convey information about important war installations to the enemy by means of a pigeon sent to them by the enemy. In future, the Courts-Martial will impose the death penalty inexorably in all cases of this nature."

To: Major B. Melland
M.I. 14(d)

JK.
28.3.44.

SECRET.

Message No. 79

SIGS. [A]—CARRIER PIGEON SERVICE.

Regent 8131/53

Pigeon No. 445   Sent from Cambridge   on 9.7.   1941
                  Returned to Barnstaple   on 12.7.   1941
With following Message in French from Calvados dated 11.7. 1941
Transmitted to M.I.14.D.M.I. & R.A.F. at   hours on 14.7. 1941

(6091D) Wt /2002 10 Pads 6/41 H, J, R & L, Ld Gp 745

We found your pigeon on the 10th July near CHEURES(?) and sent it off again early on the 11th as we were unable to keep it longer owing to there being Germans in the Commune. They have already destroyed one pigeon found by a women who gave it up to them.

The only information we can give you is that there is a munitions depot in the forest of St Ohdre near La Huquette.

The Germans hope still to invade England and their moral is till very good.

For 8 days past trains have been passing full of men, lorries and M.Gs. These trains are of 25 to 30 wagons each.

No other news to give you except to beg you to make an end to this as soon as you can before we die of hunger.

We live in the hope, like many other Frenchman, that Victory is near. Come, dear comrades of yesterday!

                                          No Signature.

SECRET.

Message No. 84

SIGS. I [A]—CARRIER PIGEON SERVICE.

Regent 8131/53

Pigeon No. DSg 69.	Sent from Cambridge	on 7th November	1941
	Returned to Aberdeen	on 10th November	1941
With following Message in Dutch		from Hoorn, N. Holland, dated 7th November	1941
Transmitted to M.I.14, & R.A.F.	at 1500	hours on 12th November	1941

Dropped at HOORN, NORTH HOLLAND, on the 7th November. Another two dropped in the neighbourhood, but they were taken to the police: Not much news about the invasion of England.
There is an oil dump and depot of Rubber Boats in the KRENTENTUIN (Currant-garden, see attached) at HOORN. Air Post on top of the Public Baths and Water Tower.
The German Morale is good. The factories in EDAM are being adapted for the manufacture of "Fokker" spare parts. Round it there is..........?
The "Fokker" factories have been well and truly hit.
Do not drop pigeons in thickly populated areas.
At SCHOUW on the N.H. (Noord Holland) Canal a good deal is being unloaded, chiefly cases with grenades, and they are stacked there in depots.
Some little while ago the auction room of van Zwaag was hit by a bomb, there was no point in that at all. Who did that?
On the Berkhouten Road there is a .... house, which at the moment is full of Germans. At ALKMAAR they are preparing the barracks at the Westerweg (Western Road) for the winter when the Germans return from Russia, and have won the war over there, ha-ha.
But boys, beware and don't underestimate him. Can't you throw any time bombs on the railways to Germany? Much too much goes there, we lose everything, so keep your eyes open. Patriotic greetings also to the Queen.

I sign

TOON.

V.

GENERAL STAFF SIGS. (A) CPS
12 NOV 1941
Ref. No.
ARMY PIGEON SERVICE

TOP SECRET.

SPECIAL SECTION (CARRIER PIGEON) R. SIGNALS (Regent 8131/53)

Message No. 947

Pigeon No. 43-93	Sent from Cambridge	on 30th July 1944
Returned to Plymouth		on 6th August 1944
Message in French	from LANGOAT (COTES DU NORD)	dated 4th Aug. 1944
Transmitted to SHAEF, M.I.14(d), A.I.1(c), N.I.D.2.	at 1000 hours	on 8th Aug. 1944

I found your pigeon on 31st July in the morning and am liberating it on 4th August at 8 o'clock in the morning in good weather.

Enemy Defences at PLOUNEZ, 2 Kms. from PAIMPOL. There are large long range guns there, surrounded by a wall of reinforced concrete. They are supplied with ammunition by the railway line which passes into the military terrain. There are also casemates there for the purpose of storing ammunition. The guns are electrically controlled. There are also large depots of gas-oil in the military terrain, ack-ack batteries and barracks for the soldiers. The whole comprises an area of 4 sq. kilometres. There are no civilians there.

At the mouth of the TRIEUX there is a naval base capable of receiving light ships such as fast corvettes and "contre-torpilleurs". The locality is called LEZARDRIEUX. Bomb the large guns and the port of LEZARDRIEUX.

At the mouth of the TRIEUX there is also a fortified island having direct access to the sea. It is called ILE A BOIS. A white house in limestone serves as a repair depot and guiding mark for the Navy.

At SERVEL in the district of LANNION there is an airfield but it is being demolished by the Boches, who are blowing up the runways and the hangars, but ack-ack guns are still there. The colours on the epaulettes of the troops who are there are grey, red, yellow.

Civilian carts are carrying material for the enemy to the station of GUINGAMP.

Listening-in installations at PERROS - GUIREC. There are also ack-ack and machine-guns there.

We listen to the radio from London and Algiers but the Boches have cut the electric current, so that we cannot hear your emissions. There are some battery sets left and instructions over the radio, or by pamphlets dropped from the air, are passed from mouth to mouth.

The morale of the Boches here is very bad. They are getting nasty and burn the farms in which young people of the resistance movement are hidden. They are also forbidding to go about on bicycles.

(Sgd) Les pommes seront bientot mures a LANGOAT.

TOP SECRET.

SPECIAL SECTION (CARRIER PIGEON) R. SIGNALS (Regent 8131/53)

Message No. 1007

Pigeon No. 40-1572 Sent from Cambridge on 11th August 1944
Returned to Woolston on 21st August 1944
Message in French from ST.JEAN DU CARDONNAY (SEINE INFERIEURE) dated 13th Aug. 1944
Transmitted to SHAEF, M.I.14(d), A.I.1(c), NID 2, at 1200 hours on 22nd Aug. 1944

Flying bombs no longer start from the ground. They are launched from aircraft immediately after night-fall. Those aircraft come from airfields in the ROUEN district.

Flying bombs no longer start from ST.JEAN.

Crosses on the attached sketch show where bombs fell on the 8th August. The sketch also gives location of ack-ack, listening post, searchlight and H.Q.

At CANTELEU there are Germans in the Chateau and five block-houses in the park of the Chateau.

At the extreme N.E. corner of ST.JEAN DU CARDONNAY there is an Etat Major in a small chalet, but no troops.

At ST.JEAN there is a small wood with ammunition, S.W., in the middle of the plain.

At the naval dockyard of TRAIT on the right hand side of the river SEINE there are two ferry-boats under construction, and one submarine which has been completed and is ready to leave. The workmen leave the dockyard at 1900 hrs. German time, and begin work in the morning at 0700 hrs.

Many troops cross the SEINE by ferries at night. The ferry of DUCLAIR has been bombed, but has not yet been touched. For further particulars see second sketch.

The morale of the Germans is very low. Troops pass here going north.

No, or very few, troops at ST.JEAN DU CARDONNAY, but there are more at ROUMARE. They are hungry and steal all they can. Many say that they will surrender.

(Sgd) R.J.

There are trenches and holes by way of defence.

4 ack-ack guns W.N.W. of DUCLAIR on hills.

Steam ferry-boat runs all night long. Bomb the left hand side of the river.

The Etat Majors have left.

Troops are beginning to go East.

Your bombing is too dispersed. The railway line BARENTIN-CAUDEBEC does not run any longer.

Jamming station at LOUVETOT between CAUDEBEC and YVETOT.

No arms or ammunition in the district of DUCLAIR.

(Sgd) Le Chef des F.F.I. Rottembourg.

2 Encls:

SECRET.		Message No. 81.
I [A]—CARRIER PIGEON SERVICE.		Regent 8131/53

Pigeon No. E 382 Sent from Cambridge on 31st October 1941
Returned to Winchester on 3rd November 1941
With following Message in French from Mr. AMIENS dated 2nd Novr. 1941
Transmitted to M.I.14 & R.A.F. at 1300 hours on 4th November 1941

a) Embarkation and disembarkation exercises of men and material on rubber boats (pneumatique) at the cycle track of ALBERT (Somme).

b) Fairly large petrol dumps at SALEUX on the left of the railway to AMIENS.

c) Some soldiers are beginning to discover the lies told by their chiefs with regard to invasion; they had been told of a crossing of 3 K.M.

d) About the 20th October an artillery train went North and others on foot by the road of ABBEVILLE (train of English and Scottish prisoners in very good condition went in the direction of ROUEN).

e) I know nothing about the aerodromes at POIX et GLISY - all I know is that runaways and modern installations are always being proceeded with - i.e. catapulting of bombers by means of a heavy cable, which rolls up on a lorry at 200 (K.M.) per hour.

f) Bombing of the Railway AMIENS - ABBEVILLE was successful. Training centre for cadet officers who are billeted with civilians at FLIXY.
General stores at PETIT ST JEAN between the station ST.ROCH, the chocolate factory and the hippodrome at AMIENS. Important stocks of grain, oats and straw.

g) In the RUE DE LA REPUBLIC at AMIENS there is a military house where the higher staff officers meet.

There are not many aeroplanes on the aerodromes and during the night there are no longer any aerial patrols as before.

Your propaganda makes fairly good progress, because one sees a good many inscriptions and V's on all the walls, but there are always bad Frenchmen, especially in the country, where peasants sell butter and eggs to the Germans at very high prices, and do not give anything to the French.

One hears many people say: What are the English waiting for before they come - there is some truth in this because there are hardly any occupational troops in this neighbourhood. In any case the majority of the French are ready to help you if you come; there are a lot of arms hidden.

I live in a little village 10 K.M. south of AMIENS.

The Radio broadcasts are jammed more and more by the Germans. Having no radio set, I cannot say anything more on the subject.

Beware of false information because yesterday morning a German veterinary picked up 2 parachutes and a little while later a patrol of about 30 soldiers together with prisoners searched the field.

Long live France and England.

Notus - 62 B.

TOP SECRET.

SPECIAL SECTION (CARRIER PIGEON) R. SIGNALS

Message No. 934 (Regent 8131/53)

Pigeon No. 43-4539.	Sent from Cambridge	on 29th Dec. 1943.
Returned to Shepherds Bush		on 1st August, 1944.
Message in French from MEAULTE (BOMES)		dated Undated 1944
Transmitted to M.I.14(d), SHAEF	at 1030	hours on 2nd Aug. 1944

14 h

    Ack-ack battery in the forest of GREVILLERS.

    MEAULTE has not been damaged.

    Come as soon as possible, because the sufferings endured by the civilian prisoners are horrible. Members of the resistance have been shot at ST. LEGER. A girl from HENIN was tied to a wheel barrow and kicked about and beaten, because she had a transmission set.

    Collaborator FRENO near CROISILLES.

    We listen to London at 1115 hrs., but it is jammed.

    We count on our early deliverance.

                         (Sgd) No. 45

Comments please
14 b
14 h
2

TOP SECRET.

SPECIAL SECTION (CARRIER PIGEON) R. SIGNALS (Regent 8131/53)

Message No. 937

Pigeon No. 39-391	Sent from Cambridge	on 30th July	1944
Returned to Oxford		on 15th August	1944
Message in French from TOTES (SEINE INFERIEURE)		dated 2nd Aug.	1944
Transmitted to CHAMP, M.I.14(d), A.I.1(c), S.P.	at 1700 hours	on 16th Aug.	1944

The railway line from DIEPPE to ROUEN was completely repaired on 3rd August between CLERES and AUFFAY. The damage caused by your many aircraft on the 18th July was very great indeed, and the aviators have aimed very accurately. Could you not destroy the railway bridge over which passes the line from the coast to ST.SAENS? That bridge is 60m south of the station ST.VICTOR l'ABBAYE. There is another bridge at 300m north of the same station. If you destroy that also, the Boches who are still in the district of DIEPPE would be cut off from all supplies, and it would be more difficult for them to move about. The branch lines from ROUEN to DIEPPE and from ROUEN via BOSC LE HARD and from LEUILLY between CLERES and ST.VICTOR l'ABBAYE are intact. If you bomb the railway line over 1 Km. you will have the chance to cut these two railway lines and to destroy the four railway bridges at that spot. During the last ten days now numerous armoured cars have used one of those bridges on the road from FRESNAY LE LONG to BOSC LE HARD.

There are two ack-ack batteries reinforced by four guns of smaller calibre between the farm of LA JOSRIE and LA HOUSSAYE - BERENGER. 600m from that farm and on the left hand side of the road going from the church of HOUSSAYE - BERENGER there are six big guns and sound apparatus. From there, going south, there are the buildings where the personnel live and also six other guns of 105 and the four small ones. All that can be found between L'ASILE DE GRUCHY and the church of LA HOUSSAYE - BERENGER. These guns have shot down at least 18 aircraft in one month.

With regard to the robots, herewith some emplacements:-

At CLERES, LE MONT CAUVAIRE on the Sports Ground of the college of NORMANDY, that is to say, between the Chateaux of the college, a small forest and the end of the farm. Runways and depots are on that ground and face north. You have nothing to fear. The ground is 60m from the Chateaux going towards CLERES. Those Chateaux are inhabited by the Boches.

/continued 2.

PTO

SECRET.

Continuation of Report No. 967 -2-

<u>At FRESQUIENNES.</u> North of the Chateau there are three departing points of the robots. They work every day. The Chateau is occupied by the Germans, and the runways and installation are 150m in the park.

<u>At ST.JEAN DU CARDONNAY, CHATEAU DE POLIGNAC.</u> Exactly the same thing. Nearly all the robots crash over the first kilometres and have caused damage and death, especially at BARENTIN in the park and in northerly direction.

Other information with regard to robots will follow by radio.

We Frenchmen would be glad if, for the purpose of bombing, you would use your famous dive-bombers, because the others make victims and cause much damage, as they are not so precise. We hope that you will understand us, because our duty is to live for our dear France, which we want to deliver from the Boches. They know that their bosses are not so sure as they were in 1940.

I would be very glad if you could let me know over the radio if the pigeon has arrived. My dear comrade, the Captain, who is also writing to you, is one of yours, and reached us from the sky. We will look after him, or rather, after them, because there are a number of them and I know them all. Till soon. It will be a pleasure to see you here.

I would be glad to receive the following message over the radio at 7.30 or 9.30 hrs:-

"Pour Le Fauve Coco est bien arrive."

Your last bombing of the railway station of MOTTEVILLE was not successful. The trains still run, and many of them.

<u>Derniere Heure.</u> If this news should fall in the hands of the Germans, I ask them to receive this message with the famous saying of Cambronne -- "Fou moi le camp."

(Sgd) Le Fauve.

<u>In English.</u>

By pigeon dropped near TOTES, night of 30/31st July. Released 2.8.44. Two other pigeons dropped at the same time were handed to the German authorities.

The following are safe and well and awaiting developments under cover.:-

F/Lt. D.M. Shanks, R.A.A.F.
W/O Capusdin, A. R.C.A.F.
Lieutenants, V.Dingman - Pensinger - Clements - Bishop - Hansen - McDonald B - U.S.A.A.F.

Please advise all concerned.

/continued 3. PTO

SECRET.

Continuation of Report No. 987 -3-

"NO BALL" at MT.CANDON, N. of BACQUEVILLE in N.E. corner of large wood; at BEITERSVILLE in garden of white mansion; at MT.CAUVERN, S. of CLERES.

Ack-ack at MT.CANDON, 3 pos. "vierflakke" in fields to north of wood. 2 in woods.

Other "NO BALL" being constructed at various points but are mobile within a few days. New type in use; does not seem to have catapult take-off. Old type to start, run up motor, fire charge in catapult, take off with full motor and jettison iron wheels 8 in diam., 8 in wide, about ½ min after.

Ack-ack pos. 5 heavy, 6 Kms. S.S.W. of ST.VICTOR l'ABBAYE. Other pos. of 12 heavy destroyed by 18 fighter-bombers 0630 hrs. 8.7.44., after bringing down 2 Forts. Some of crew safe, as above.

Aircraft. German aircraft fly every night at dusk very, very low - tree-top level from East to West over AUFFAY - TOTES area - 177.88.190 identified, but not many of each, 30 odd 190, are uncertain.

Army. About 100 infantry on bicycles went through AUFFAY from DIEPPE ? on morning of 17 July and crossed SEINE near CAUDEBEC by boat - Sunday morning, 30th July, 80 horses went through (with light artillery ? - local talk. I saw horses, not guns) to ROUEN.

The road ST.VICTOR l'ABBAYE to CLERES carries only staff cars and French supplies; very seldom convoys of military importance. The railway near AUFFAY is nearly mended and is expected to run on Thursday, 3rd August. They say that a lot of infantry went south on foot in the night of 6th July, but were not on this road. They are using horses by night to move a lot of supplies south. Most horses requisitioned from farms.

Bombing. The use of heavy bombers at high levels on "NO BALL" and other pin-point targets is to be deplored as they very, very seldom hit any military targets, but do a great deal of damage to French property and make many enemies. An instance; on the afternoon of 14th July, many Lancs. came over and bombed above cloud. The markers went down near the little factory △, but the heavies let go up to five miles off and bombs fell uselessly in the fields and villages and caused much damage. I saw at least ten sticks fall that did no military good whatever. All the locals ask for Lightning F/B and Mosquito F/B on the "NO BALL" and flak targets.

/continued 4.

PTO

SECRET.

Continuation of Report No. 987

On the roads the fighters are hitting a lot of French civilian traffic, but are doing good work keeping the Hun quiet.

Morale. Huns very tired of war and frightened. They mutter "Tommy vient" and have no heart.

When "NO BALL" started an old sergeant told me "London kaputt 96 hours", but a week later said the bomb was a failure. Of the first four fired from one position two fell within 200 yards off position, the third not far off. Many fall on starting and can be heard exploding. The average rate of fire seems to be less than one shot per installation per day here.

If you could send further pigeons, please drop them in the cultivations between ST.VICTOR l'ABBAYE – MONTREUIL and BOSMELET. A 1/50,000 map of this part of the country would be very acceptable.

On the night of 1st–2nd August, troops on foot and horse transport passed, going south.

If you have any instructions for any of the above-named they will be received if sent by the usual channel or the radio. The use of bicycles or trains is impossible and we are advised not to try to cross the borders to Spain or Switzerland. We are told to wait here for "Monty".

(Sgd) Obus

Comments please.

M.I.14 (b)
(h)
(A)
(d)

TOP SECRET.

SPECIAL SECTION (CARRIER PIGEON) R. SIGNALS

Message No. 902 (Regent 8131/53)

Pigeon No. .... Sent from .... on 1944
Returned to H.M.S. Mayflower in the Channel on 8th July 1944
Message in French from SEINE INFERIEURE dated 7th July 1944
Transmitted to SHAEF, M.I.14(d), A.I.1(e) at 1730 hours on 13th July 1944

To the Minister of War,

I was very happy to find your pigeon and herewith send you the following information.

Round where I live I know of 4 emplacements of flying torpedoes.

1. One in the CHATEAU DE MOTTEVILLE, opposite the station in the avenue.
2. One at ENULEVILLE (? AUGIVILLE) in the avenue of the Chateau.
3. One in the avenue of the Chateau FREQUIENT (? FRESQUIENNE)
4. One in the avenue of the Chateau DE ST.JEAN DU CARDONNAY.

Ack-ack at LA HOUSSAYE BERENGER near the coast.

Some trains still pass along the line PARIS - HAVRE.

Many troops are coming from the SOMME to fortify the length of the SEINE.

I listen every day to your news bulletins.

The Germans in my district are very demoralised and wear no colour on their epaulettes.

Please advise me over the radio if the pigeon has safely arrived, and say -

"Le Poupart qui aime sa cherie est bien rentré par le mauvais temps."

Vive l'Angleterre. Vive la France.   A bas l'Allemagne.

Marginal notes: h, 15

Comments please
M.I.14h
15 (b)
d.

The next several documents include comments about the value of the messages as military intelligence.

File COLUMBA

SECRET CIPHER TELEGRAM

an example of information of operational value from source COLUMBA (message 253)

From : The War Office.
To : Freedom, ALGIERS.

Desp. 1630 1 Dec. 42.

IMPORTANT.

83424 cipher (M.I.14) dated 1 Dec.
    For MOCKLER FERRYMAN.

Begins. Source of uncertain value reports Brenner railway blocked 15 - 20 Nov. due sabotage. Traffic resumed 20 Nov. and units Leibstandarte Adolf Hitler passed to Italy. Whole division believed due go to ROME. Comment. We have indications division still in North France (ST. LO area) 21 Nov. Move to Italy therefore not (repeat not) yet accepted but possibility not excluded. Ends.

T.O.O.1145A/1.

C.6 (Telegrams).

NB Columba

Copies to:- M.I.3(a).
              M.I.3(b).
              M.I.14.
              M.I.17.

MOST SECRET

ANNEXE B.

VALUATIONS.

From G.H.Q., Home Forces June, 1943.

In forwarding this month's suggestions for source Columba, it is desired to state how highly this source is appreciated. It will become increasingly valuable as the time for operations approaches. It is very much to be hoped that Columba's range and resources will be continually increased.

From A.I. 1(e). 17.8.43.

Thank you very much for your Pigeon Report No.486. This report is most interesting to me and has been very useful.

I have already shown it to the Secretary of State for Air, the Deputy Chief of the Air Staff and the C. in C. of Bomber Command and I am making some copies of it for them.

From my point of view, the Pigeon Service produces occasional extremely valuable reports and this is one of them.

Yours sincerely,

(Sgd) R.V. Jones.

A.D.I. Science.

From S.O.E. 8.12.43.

Dear Kleyn,

I would like to send a word of appreciation for all the good work you have done, and are still doing, for us.

Although the percentage of success has not been so high as both you and we could have wished — mostly due to atmospheric conditions, and other reasons, such as parachutes not opening and birds going astray through wind draft — I feel that the results obtained have been well worth while. They have certainly proved invaluable to P.W.E. and to ourselves.

The demands from the Field are increasing, and I trust that we shall continue in the close collaboration which has existed between us in the past.

Yours sincerely,

(Sgd) R.I. Dobson,
Major.

From P.I.D. 9.12.43.

On the extracts we receive we should like to offer the following remarks:-

(a) The information contained in these extracts does not duplicate information from other sources.

(b) The messages have this unique advantage over practically all other sources that they are speedy and detailed with regard to geographical location.

(c) The matters which are always of interest to us and which form in many ways an essential part of our intelligence are:-

/ (i)...

- 2 -

(i) Information regarding the audibility and reactions to the B.B.C.

(ii) Living conditions.

(iii) The names of collaborators.

In almost all the information there is something falling into the above categories, and we wish to put on record the usefulness of this service. It is all the more important as the Region which it normally covers is one which is not covered by other sources of information in the same detail, and it would be a great loss to lose this particular service. We have already noted its absence during the past few weeks, perhaps due to operational difficulties.

(Sgd) L.J. Beck,

C.I.O., French Region

From B.B.C. 13.12.43.

Dear Capt. Kleyn,

In reviewing our work for this half year we find that we are indebted to your service for over sixty very useful messages from Western Europe and would like to express our appreciation. Not only are these reports unique as representing almost the only source of detailed information to reach the B.B.C. within a day or two of dispatch from that end, but they have also furnished us constantly with up-to-date news which has proved of real practical value both to our Editorial and to our Technical Staffs.

Our French Intelligence Section say that they find these messages "of the utmost value, as they so frequently provide an advance indication of listeners' reactions to particular news of particular items broadcast – reactions which would otherwise reach us too late to be taken into account". Criticisms and requests received so quickly by this particular channel are also of the greatest help. The same applies to our Belgian Section.

The Engineering Division also write to record their appreciation of the information about reception: "it is a great help to us to get really up-to-date news from places where we otherwise have to wait sometimes months for reports from other sources – we shall be glad to go on receiving these reports as often as possible."

We thank you and all concerned sincerely for all this much appreciated help.

Yours sincerely,

(Sgd) Jonathan Griffin

European Intelligence Director.

The deployment by the Germans of hawks, falcons, and snipers to kill the pigeons and the German use of decoy pigeons suggests the Columba messages had value as intelligence. The narrator of the documentary *The War of the Birds* explains that decoy pigeons were German pigeons trained to fly back to German lofts and outfitted with counterfeit British message capsules and rings. The British used decoy pigeons too. These were British pigeons trained to fly back to British lofts and outfitted with counterfeit German message capsules and rings. The following report tells more about decoy pigeons and the German response to Operation Columba.

C O L U M B A

ANNEXE C

Enemy Reaction:

Enemy reaction may be divided into four categories:-

(A) Regulations and inflictions of penalties for the civilian population of occupied territories.

(B) The capture of as many of our pigeons as possible.

(C) The employment and encouragement of breeding of hawks and falcons, and marksmen.

(D) Dropping decoy German pigeons.

(A) **Regulations and inflictions of penalties for the civilian population of occupied territories.**

Immediately after the occupation of Denmark, Norway, Holland, Belgium and France, the Germans took steps to control the activity of pigeon owners and breeders, and this control has been tightened up at frequent intervals. It took the following form:

BELGIUM. July 1942. Source - M.I. 19 (R.P.S.)/971 dated 10.9.42

The Belgian Federation of Pigeon Experts (FEDERATION DES COLOMBOPHILES) has been made responsible to the German Governor General for every matter concerning pigeons in Belgium, although certain duties and responsibilities have been put on local authorities as an additional safeguard.

For example, the Federation keeps the register of every pigeon in the country. As an additional safeguard every owner must send in a return of the birds he possesses once monthly to his local commune.

Furthermore every owner must keep a duplicate list of his birds, one copy of which must be affixed to the door of the pigeon loft, and the other kept in his house or office.

This list must give the number of the ring on every pigeon. The Federation has a list of these numbers and every ring issued is duly registered. Informant is sure that the Germans check this register, that the Federation must give all information required, and that a copy of the register may even be in the hands of the Germans.

The control is not only very strict but penalties for any infraction of the regulations are most severe. Long terms of imprisonment, and even the death sentence, may be imposed if any activity against the safety of the occupying forces is suspected.

The lists and pigeon lofts are liable to police control at any moment, either by the Belgians or by the Germans, or by both Belgian and German police acting together.

It was strictly forbidden to let pigeons make any flights. They were sometimes seen in the country but should a bird with a ring be caught or shot the owner would have serious trouble.

22.10.43. Source OX 22432/IV/24845. Notice displayed at Ivoir on 16.9.43 - "The Occupying Authority asks us to communicate the following:- 'The kommandantur will pay a premium up to 625 Belgian francs to those inhabitants who will deliver to the kommandantur carrier pigeons released by the enemy from the air.'"

/6.6.43 ...

- 2 -

6.6.43. Source "Daily Express" - 'Julien Ferrant, a Belgian, has been executed for trying to send messages by carrier pigeon to the Allies'.

HOLLAND. 19.7.41. Source - "Nieuwsblad van het Noorden" - 'Carrier pigeons and ordinary pigeons may only be kept if the owners are members of unions. It is not allowed to let pigeons fly freely or keep them aboard ships. Jews and foreigners must not keep pigeons. Pigeons must not be sold, exchanged or given away. The Burgomaster is responsible that un-owned pigeons are killed. The decree is in force from August 4th.'

21.7.43. "Deutsche Zeitung in den Niederlanden" reports that the Deutsches Landegericht recently brought a case against the shoemaker, Adrianus Gerardus Valk, from Udenhout, who was not only guilty of not slaughtering 13 carrier pigeons, in spite of regulations, but has unnecessarily tortured them, cutting off one foot from each and handing the ring in to the authorities, in order to deceive them about the fact that they had been done away with. In view of the brutality of his conduct, Valk was sentenced to one year's imprisonment.

19.8.43. - Source - pigeon message No. 506 dated 20.8.43. (Holland). The message says "Rear a couple of young pigeons for me. I have had to kill all mine".

18.10.43. - Source - "Nationale Dagblad", Utrecht. The German Landegericht in a three-days session at Vught, sentenced many Brabant and Limburg carrier pigeon owners, who nearly always stated that they had kept their pigeons, because they could not part from them. As in most cases there was no ill-will on the part of the pigeon owners they were usually sentenced to a minimum of three months' imprisonment with deduction of preventive custody.

NORWAY. 11.10.41. - Source - Moscow. "According to a decree issued by Terboven, the keeping of pigeons has been prohibited in Norway as from the 10th, October, 1941. All pigeons have to be killed off. At the same time, the Norwegians have to deliver rings from the pigeons' feet at police stations."

19.11.41. - Source - Oslo. "The German armed forces appeal to the Norwegian civilian population to hand over at once foreign carrier pigeons and everything connected with them to the nearest Defence Station. A reward of 60 Kronen will be paid for each carrier pigeon, and 80 Kronen for anything found in connection with the pigeons."

DENMARK. 2.7.42. - Source - "Flensburger Nachrichten". The newspaper published a notification to the effect that near the Danish frontiers it is prohibited to release carrier pigeons, and that, as all pigeons flying free belong to the Wehrmacht, it is prohibited to shoot them.

FRANCE. 16.7.43. - Source - "La Petite Gironde" published the following warning:-

'We wish to remind the civil population that the keeping of carrier-pigeons is a punishable offence. Anyone finding a carrier-pigeon must bring it, and any notes attached, direct to the Town Hall or to the nearest German authorities. The Wehrmacht will give rewards up to the sum of 1,000 fr. for the delivery of these carrier-pigeons or leaflets dropped by parachute.'

20.11.43. – Source – "Le petit Dauphinois". A decree published on November 19th. obliges owners to declare all carrier pigeons to mayors before the morning of November 21st by giving a triplicate list of ring numbers. All future changes

/in ...

- 3 -

in the numbers of pigeons owned are to be similarly declared. This applies to all pigeons capable of carrying news, for instance, tumblers and those having received awards for competitions. The decree also forbids the keeping of any sort of carrier pigeons in the following departments: Basses-Pyrenees, Haute-Garonne, Ariege, Pyrenees-Orientales, Aude, Herault, Bouches-du-Rhone, Corsica, Savoie, Haute-Savoie, Alpes-Maritimes, Var, Basses-Alpes, and Hautes-Alpes. In all other departments dove-cots must remain closed.

19.11.43. – Source – "Evening Standard". 'All carrier pigeons in Vicy must be declared by their owners before Sunday, according to Paris report, of 19.11.43. Failure to do so entails a penalty of 1-5 years' imprisonment and £10-£50 fine.'

It is clear from the above that from the beginning the Germans were fully alive to "pigeon possibilities". By our dropping some 9,000 pigeons on occupied Europe between April 1941 and December 1943, they can hardly have become less pigeon-minded considering that a large percentage of that number has fallen into their hands, as evidenced by the following examples:-

Pigeon Report No. 9. 14.5.41. Courtrai. Pigeons picked up by Germans.

Pigeon Report No. 39. 11.7.41. Calvados. Germans destroyed one given up by a woman.

Pigeon Report No. 51. 18.7.41. Calvados. Pigeons in Avranches area in hands of enemy. The mayor of Aunay (half-boche) handed over the pigeon.

Pigeon Report No. 52. 22.7.41. St. Germain le Vasson. Two pigeons taken by the enemy.

Pigeon Report No. 60. 7.8.41. Waereghem. Two pigeons handed to police. 250 fr. reward.

Pigeon Report No. 61. 7.8.41. Vive St. Bavon. One pigeon in hands of police. July '41.

Pigeon Report No.69.   -.8.41.   St.Germain.   Pigeon landed there and handed to police at Conde.

Pigeon Report No.81.   2.11.41.   Amiens.   Two parachutes picked up by 30 soldiers, who searched the field.

Pigeon Report No.263.   21.11.43.   Wavre.   Parachuted pigeon found in lake between Wavre and Gastoche.   Germans advised of this and they seized it.

Pigeon Report No.298.   18.7.43.   Farmer took pigeon to kommandantur.

Pigeon Report No.305.   17.4.43.   Vimoutieres gendarmes took pigeons to police at Alencon.

Pigeon Report No.344.   18.5.43.   Pas de Calais.   Various pigeons in hands of gendarmes.

Pigeon Report No.390.   15.6.43.   Merdrignac.   Pigeon fell on wires in Merdrignac.   Four Bothes arrived and took it.

Pigeon Report No.460.   18.7.43.   Mariembourg.   The mayor too the pigeons to the Boches.

Pigeon Report No.535.   25.8.43.   Ploermel.   Many pigeons have fallen in the town and are in the hands of German sentries at Ploermel.

/Pigeon ...

- 4 -

Pigeon Report No.545.   1.9.43.   Florennes.   An Italian found one of your pigeons and killed it.   The coward!

On 26.2.43. the Germans collected a cage suspended to a small parachute and containing four pigeons, at a place called Laarbeekbosch near Brussels. - Source - CX 222000/IV/13746.

At Laroche and Rendeux, pigeons and parachutes were found on 29.7.42 by the Germans. - Source 12.

A parachute carrying leaflets and a request for information regarding certain coastal defences came down in the Florennes area.   It fell into the hands of the Rexists who handed it over to the Germans. The request for information was accompanied by a pigeon. - Source - CX 99211/IV/1059. 15.11.42.

19.8.42. P.I.D. Censorship. Extract from the Bolivia newspaper 'O Tiempo' of 17.5.42. This report is supposed to come from Vichy to the effect that British airmen drop carrier pigeons by means of parachutes, each bearing a container in which was a questionnaire, and a request that the French people should answer the questions, put the paper into the container again and release the pigeon, which was in a small cage.

Most of the people who found baskets of pigeons dropped by 'planes after the Dieppe raid did fill in the notes and return them. A few handed them over to the Germans, in the hope of securing the release of prisoners. - Source CX 27435/IV/757 dated 6.11.42.

On 29.7.42. cardboard cylindrical boxes attached to parachutes containing pigeons, a small box of maize and a note giving instructions, were found in the fields near Chimay (Belgium). Three individuals who found them took them to the gendarmerie. They were delivered to the Germans who sent the pigeons off with false information. Other pigeons were picked up by civilians, who sent them back with true information - Source - CX 22432/IV/66, dated 18.10.42.

A number of pigeons which were dropped in the region of Hirson in the night of 15th-16th September 1943 were taken to the Feldgendarmerie. - Source - CX 22432/IV/26449, dated 7.11.43.

Apart from the foregoing, it must be borne in mind that quite a considerable number of aircraft carrying pigeons have not returned. It is not known whether all these aircraft were voluntarily or involuntarily destroyed, but it may be assumed that the Germans have had an opportunity to collect evidence that pigeons were being carried.

Considering all, there can be no doubt that the Germans are fully aware of our pigeon activities.

(B) <u>The capture of as many of our pigeons as possible.</u>

Apart from regulations and the infliction of penalties, there is evidence to show that the Germans have to do a good deal of running about and searching to collect as many pigeons as they can.

Pigeon Report No.442 eminating from Gace (Orne) dated

25.6.43 states:- "With regard to parachutists, please note the very methodical organisation of the Germans by rapid and numerous patrols in motor cars, side-cars, and carriages."

Pigeon Report No.547 emanating from Loudun (Vienne) dated 16.8.43. states:- "I want to advise you that many of your parachuted pigeons have fallen in the hands of the Germans who were warned by the observation post after the aircraft had passed overhead. An hour afterwards 150 Boches arrived in motor cars, and they searched gardens, paddocks and looked on the roofs and made enquiries in many houses. People were arrested and searched, and I think that finally they found four".

Considering the wide area covered, the dropping of our pigeons may contribute in a small way to a kind of a German-invented nerve war.

(C) <u>The employment and encouragement of breeding of hawks and falcons, and marksmen.</u>

It will be remembered that during the 1870-1 Seige of Paris pigeons carried numerous messages from the City over the German lines. Germans trained hawks to intercept the messengers.

We have first-class evidence that they are doing the same thing today. Even if those birds of prey are not trained (i.e. take back their quarry), it is fair to assume that the Germans encourage the breeding of hawks and falcons along the coastline of Europe.

A British officer took two pigeons on a Commando raid on 4.9.43., and at 0630 hrs. released it from the coast of France. (Radio silence was essential). As soon as the two birds were released, and not more than 60 yds. away from him a swarm of falcons descended from the cliffs, and attacked and killed both pigeons.

Pigeon Report No.376 of May 1943, emanating from Doullens states:- "Marksmen on the coast endeavour to shoot down pigeons from time to time."

(D) <u>Dropping decoy German pigeons.</u>

Pigeon Report No.376 of May 1943 emanating from Doullens states:- "I do not sign because the Germans also drop carrier pigeons, which you must understand take the messages to the kommandantur. Various patriots who wrote their names and addresses have been arrested."

Pigeon Report No.394, June 1943 (destination not known probably North France) states:-
"I know that those gentlemen also drop pigeons."

Pigeon Report No.634, dated 7.11.43. from Bayeux states:-
"I am not anxious to keep your pigeon a long time. You will understand why. I do not give you my name or the locality where I live, in case the pigeon might have been changed for a German pigeon, and I distrust the Boches."

Summing Up.

It may be taken as established that the Germans are fully pigeon-minded, and that our continued activities can hardly make them more so.

Considering the area concerned, it is unlikely, however, that they have an accurate idea how many pigeons we send over and any increase or decrease would hardly be noticeable, unless for reasons of deception or otherwise it were decided at any given moment to "sow thickly" in a small particular locality.

There is no evidence to show that the Germans do the same thing over this country. They, of course, have no friendly population here, so that they would appear to have no answer to our pigeon activities. A watch is kept, as far as is conveniently possible, over our coasts for pigeons flying out.

That their reaction has hardly ever taken the form of "planting" information on us, and never that of placing some sort of explosive in containers, remains a surprise, considering the number of birds that have fallen into their hands. One can hardly suppose that their small meat ration has something to do with this!

Occasionally a foreign-owned bird falls into our hands. In October a Dutch bird with a German practice message landed, exhausted, on board one of our ships at sea. It has been nursed back to full strength and is being dropped over Holland from the air with a "plant". Reaction, if any, will be awaited.

            (Sgd) J.L. KLEIN
                Capt.

Wing Huse
12 Dec 43.

Imagine living under the German occupation. Everything produced in the factories goes to the German army. The Germans can force you to do anything. You are starving because your country's food goes to the German army. You have seen the Jews taken away. You know people who have been killed or wounded by inaccurate Allied bombings. Imagine the sadness, the anger, the fear, the frustration, the feeling of helplessness.

Then, you find a pigeon! You have a chance to help the Allies do damage to the Germans. You have a chance to describe the horrors you see and endure. You have the hope of hearing on the BBC that the pigeon made it back with your message. You write. You are no longer helpless. You have thoughts and useful information. But you don't have much time. You must send the pigeon as soon as possible. If a friend or family member sees the pigeon they might report you to the Germans. When it is time, you toss the pigeon into the air. He circles once to get his bearings and then flies towards Britain with your words.

Bibliography

Bailey, Roderick, in association with the Imperial War Museum. *Forgotten Voices of the Secret War, An Inside History of Special Operations During the Second World War.* Ebury Press, an imprint of Ebury Publishing, 2008.

Interview with John Douglas Charrot, Imperial War Museum Collections, catalog number IWM (291630).

Interview with Frank Cromwell Griffiths, Imperial War Museum Collections, catalog number IWM (12270).

Long, David. *The Animals' VC.* Preface Publishing, an imprint of The Random House Group Limited, 2012.

Osman, Major W. H. *Pigeons in World War II.* The Racing Pigeon Publishing Co. Ltd. London, 1950.

The War of the Birds. Atlantic Productions, 2005.

Catalog numbers of images reproduced by courtesy of The National Archives, Kew in the order in which they appear:

WO208/3560 file 53 (cover)
WO 208/3555 file 65 and 66
WO 208/3556 file 2
WO 208/3560 file 70 and 71
WO 208/3560 file 22
WO 208/3560 file 44
WO 208/3555 file 42
WO 208/3562 file 6
WO 208/3560 file 78
WO 208/3560 file 13
WO 208/3555 file 39
WO 208/3555 file 70
WO 208/3560 file 16
WO 208/3555 file 45
WO 208/3555 file 78, 79, 80, and 81
WO 208/3555 file 86
WO 208/3562 file 11
WO 208/3556 file 63 and 64
WO 208/3556 file 65, 66, 67, 68, 69, and 70

Suggested Reading

Bailey, Roderick, in association with the Imperial War Museum. *Forgotten Voices of D-Day.* Ebury Press, an imprint of Ebury Publishing, 2009.

Hawthorne, Peter. *The Animal Victoria Cross-The Dickin Medal.* Pen & Sword Military, an imprint of Pen & Sword Books, Ltd., 2012.

Racing Pigeon Pictorial International World War I Tribute, #528, 2014.

The photograph of the pigeon on page 35 was taken by Dora Truong. To see more of her photographs and to read more documents about the World War II pigoens, you can visit http://worldwar2militaryintelligence.blogspot.com/